Dog Training Made Simple

A Professional Trainer Shares Her Secrets

Carol Miller

Liability Disclaimer

By reading this document, you assume all risks associated with using the advice given below, with a full understanding that you, solely, are responsible for anything that may occur as a result of putting this information into action in any way, and regardless of your interpretation of the advice.

This book is intended for educational purposes only and does not replace a consultation with a certified animal behaviorist, veterinarian, or other qualified animal professional.

Dog Training Made Simple

A Professional Trainer
Shares Her Secrets

Table of Contents

Part I – Understanding Dog Training

Introduction – What makes a well-behaved pet dog?

If you were to ask several people what makes a well-behaved dog, you would almost certainly get quite different answers. For some, a well-behaved dog is one that doesn't chew up their furniture, while for others the dog should obey every command they give her. But most people would agree that a well-behaved dog should have a basic set of reliable behaviors like "Sit" and "Come", as well as be trustworthy around food or shoes, not jump all over their guests, let them eat dinner in peace, not drag them down the street, and such.

This book sets forth a plan for teaching these basics to almost any dog. However, if your dog is showing aggression towards you, other people, or animals, please consult a professional. Aggression is growling (except during play), guarding food, people or possessions such as toys or bones, attacking people or animals, out of control barking, and lunging at other people or dogs while on a walk. Such things are beyond the scope of this book, and require specialized training plans.

Dog Training: Simple but not always easy.

If you are reading this, congratulations! You are one of the few dog owners who recognizes the importance of teaching your pet dog how to live successfully in a human world. We ask an awful lot of our dogs – I am constantly amazed at how agreeable they are about it. After all, in the natural world, everything is a chew toy, any absorbent surface is a great toilet, and they are free to roam and sniff as they please. To learn "chew this not that", "go potty here not there", "stop whatever fun thing you're doing and come here this minute" – these are fabulous feats for an animal!

Be sure to recognize just how much they have learned so far, and prepare for a fun journey of building your relationship with your dog while you train her. And keep in mind that every time you and your dog interact, one of you is training the other – I always tell my students to make sure it's you doing the training!

Determine your own goals.

Before you begin a training program, it is a good idea to think about what you are looking for. This will probably change as your dog gets better at doing what you ask, but you should give a little thought to what your own feelings about training are.

Do you want your dog to always do exactly what you ask, the first time, every time? If so, you should expect to put a lot of time into working with your dog. In dog training, as in most of life, you get out of it what you put in. If you expect amazing results, which are entirely possible, you have to accept that you will need to dedicate a good deal of your time with your dog to building up to that level.

Think of it like learning a musical instrument – no one expects to play at concert level without a major commitment to practicing. And not just practicing, but also learning new skills and educating yourself. So if you expect perfection from your dog, you will need to do the work. For most people, this kind of perfection isn't necessary. But having solid responses to these 10 behaviors will make your life with your dog much better, so consider the training time you put in as a great investment. You won't need to work at it much once she reaches the level you are happy with, and you'll reap tons of benefits.

Always keep relationship in mind.

As you work with your dog, you have the opportunity to build trust and respect. As your dog learns to pay attention and follow your lead, she will be more and more willing to do whatever you ask. Unfortunately, some training methods are based on force and intimidation, and although you can get results this way, your relationship with your dog (isn't relationship why we have dogs in the first place?) will suffer.

This training program is based on Positive Reinforcement Training methods, with no force, intimidation, punishment or other scary techniques. With these techniques you will create a dog who wants to work with you, who enjoys training, and is happy and relaxed around you.

About this book.

You will find the steps for training each behavior to be somewhat repetitive in nature. This is deliberate, for two reasons:

first, if you only want to work on some or even one of the behaviors, you may not have read the earlier instructions; and
second, it is good to understand that there are similarities in
training which may help you apply the techniques to other behaviors you want to teach your dog.

Part II - Training Basics

Positive Reinforcement Training: What is it and how does it work?

Positive Reinforcement Training was developed from decades of scientific study of how animals learn. To me, it's fascinating to see that we humans, as animals, respond to the same methods. Positive Reinforcement Training is based on the understanding that animals will do more of something if it is rewarding to them, and less of it if it is not.

This powerful knowledge can be used to shape how your dog behaves. You simply need to take control of your dog's reinforcers, or things that they want, and you can begin to control your dog. Then it's simply a matter of teaching them how you want them to act and building habits of obedience.

Motivation: How do we create it?

When we talk about motivation, we mean what creates the willingness of your dog to do what you ask. If you haven't provided any motivation (reason to do it), your dog may choose to ignore you. Your job as a trainer (and you are a dog trainer if you are training your dog), is to figure out how to motivate your dog to do what you ask, and then work on it to build a habit of obedience, so motivation becomes internal for the dog – she simply wants to do it.

Right now, stop reading and go get some paper and pencil or pen, and begin to make a list of things that are important to your dog. This can include simple things like a belly rub or treat (be sure to list what kind of treats), and also bigger things like going for a walk or a ride in the car. List toys your dog loves, activities, food, games – anything your dog thinks is fun or tasty. The bigger your list, the more motivators you have in your arsenal.

And from now on, no more freebies – these things must be earned by doing something, even if it's as simple as sitting nicely in front of you. The better you are about not giving away your rewards (that's what these things are while you are training your dog), the faster your dog will start paying attention and doing what you ask. This is often called the "Premack Principle", or "Grandma's Rule" – eat your vegetables and then you can have dessert. See how these principles apply to people too?

Just remember that your dog has to like these things. Just because you love to pet her doesn't mean she necessarily loves it. Watch her while you pet her and make sure she is enjoying it. The same goes for treats. Some dogs love cheese while others don't. Test different treats to see which are things your dog will merely eat if you give it to her versus ones she absolutely adores. Be sure to note which is which on your list.

The treat thing: Do we need to use treats forever?

No and yes. No, you won't need to use them if you follow my instructions on "weaning" off of treats. Yes, in so much as I hope you will always want to reward your dog sometimes when she's done a good job. It's sort of like a paycheck for your dog.

We want to switch to using mostly "real life rewards" like going outside, getting a belly rub, throwing a ball, and playing a game, but it's fun to treat your dog sometimes, and it will help to keep up her enthusiasm if she knows that sometimes she might earn a great treat.

Note: treats should be soft, easy-to-eat tiny pieces of something your dog likes.

Most commercial dog treats are way too large for training – each piece should be a taste for your dog. You don't want to fill her up, so cut treats into very small pieces. If you feel you are feeding your dog a lot of treats during day (Good for you! You've been working!), cut back a bit on her meals.

Some dogs love their kibble enough that you can use her regular food for basic training (not when you need high-value treats, however). You can simply measure out her food in the morning and use it to train her during the day.

Age and learning: Understanding what your dog can realistically do.

If you are beginning to train a young puppy (Good for you!), you will find that she can learn to do all of the behaviors in this book. However, puppies are like small children – the younger they are, the shorter their attention span and ability to focus.

Don't expect that your puppy will be able to do a 5 minute stay while you leave the room until she is older. As you work with her, you will be able to stretch her abilities, but don't try to make her do things she simply isn't capable of yet. Pay attention to her progress and stretch her abilities as she seems ready. Keep with it as she grows, and it will be easy to see solid results over time.

For those with an adolescent dog (7 months or so to 2-3 years), you are dealing with a teenager. Teenaged dogs have loads of enthusiasm, but a tendency to lose focus and go off and explore the world. Many dogs of this age simply can't keep their head in the game if something else is going on, so stay with the basics longer and create a super strong foundation, which will make it easier for your dog to stay focused on the task at hand as you gradually add distractions.

This is an important time to be sure your dog listens, so stay with it – you should have years ahead to enjoy the results of this work. When your dog shows she can work at the current level you are teaching, it's time to make it a bit harder.

Stages of learning: Kinda got it (beginning), Got it when nothing much else is happening (intermediate), Got it no matter what (expert).

One of the biggest mistakes people make when training their dog is to assume the job is done too soon. When you have just taught your dog something (for example "Sit"), very quickly she will be responding nicely to your command. What you must keep in mind is that she is really making her best guess as to what will get her a reward.

If you keep practicing and rewarding, she will soon pass from the "kinda got it" stage into the "got it as long as nothing else interesting is going on" stage. At this point, she can reliably sit when asked, provided there are no other people in the room, she's not outside where she has a world of smells, sights and sounds to pay attention to, there's nothing interesting on the floor, etc. etc. etc. You might say that she will easily do it for you as long as there is nothing strong pulling her away from you. Important: the stronger you train this foundation, the easier it will be for your dog to handle distractions as you train them.

To move into the next stage takes more work. You must systematically teach her that she not only can but wants to pay attention when other things are in her environment. Doing this successfully involves stepping through the levels of difficulty as opposed to jumping up to hard levels without the steps in between.

Let's go back to our "Sit" example. Your dog can easily sit when asked in the living room when you are alone and no toys are out. You now add a small distraction, and reward her nicely for being able to sit during this. A small distraction might be your spouse in the room sitting quietly in a chair not looking at the dog. When she performs a sit on command like this 8 times out of 10, you can make it a bit harder. Your spouse might stand up near where your dog is. They might make a small movement. They might make a quiet noise.

As your dog succeeds 8 times out of 10 for each of these things, you can make it slightly harder. In a relatively short period of time you can move through quite a few levels, but if you had skipped the steps, your dog might not be able to perform correctly. You want to go slowly enough that she says to herself, "Oh, it's just like the last time I did it, only slightly harder. I can do that!"

Eventually you can reach a point where your dog will respond any time, any place – provided that you have trained her to do so. Don't worry too much about this – the process for each command is laid out in detail later in this book.

Types of Training: Luring, Capturing, Shaping, and Modeling.

We will primarily use luring and shaping in this program, but we may also need to use capturing. We will NOT be using modeling.

Luring – using a piece of food or a toy to "lure" or lead a dog into a position. Very handy for "Sit", "Down" and some tricks. It is critical that, once the dog begins to catch on to what you want her to do, you stop using a lure and reward her after the behavior is performed. This will be discussed in depth later on.

Capturing – waiting for the dog to naturally do what you want, then rewarding her for it. Since dogs do what gets them rewards, soon she will be repeating the behavior in an attempt to win a treat. This can be a slower way to get a behavior, but some dogs simply won't be lured into a "Down" position, and capturing is often the simplest way to teach the command.

Shaping – a training method that involves letting the dog experiment in an attempt to get treats, sort of playing the "hot and cold" game. Example: you want your dog to touch an object with her nose. You put the object on the floor, and treat her when she looks at it. If she takes a step toward it you treat again, and continue to "shape" her behaviors by rewarding actions that are getting progressively closer to what you want. It's a very fun game for both owners and dogs, and can teach fairly complex behaviors quickly.

Modeling – this is the old-fashioned way of pushing the dog into position. There are a few problems with this. One, the dog isn't actually doing it – you are doing it for her. Two, when you push down, the dog's own instincts force her to push against you, keeping her from easily going into the position. Three, rather than have your dog figure out what you want from a cooperative point of view, you are forcing her to do something. This method is not good for your relationship, and doesn't work as well as if she can get it on her own through other means. We will not be using modeling in this program.

Clicker/Marker Training Basics

In this program I will be using Marker Training, which is the same as Clicker Training except that you use a word like "Yes!" instead of a clicking sound. If you wish to use a clicker, just substitute "click" when you read "mark". I believe that a clicker is more effective than a verbal marker, but I've found that most of my clients have too much to manage without trying to handle a clicker as well.

First, you must understand that the "mark" is not a "good dog" or praise kind of thing. It is a clear indication to your dog that what she did at the exact moment she heard the mark was what you were looking for, and will earn her a treat. The mark is always paired with a treat, and will be shortened to M/T, meaning "mark and treat your dog". At first your dog will not know that's what you mean, but she will figure it out quickly, and will begin to try to guess what she needs to do to get you to M/T.

You can see from this that your timing will be critical to your dog's understanding of what you want. If she does a sit for you when asked and you wait until she begins to get up again to M/T, she will probably think that "Sit" means "Sit and get up", or maybe just the get up part. You have confused her and slowed her learning down.

You can work on your timing by bouncing a tennis ball and saying your marker word as the ball hits the floor. Also, before you begin a training session, have a clear idea of what you are looking for, so you know what to mark.

To mark a behavior, at the exact moment she does what you are asking, say "Yes!" and give her a treat. The mark gives you time to hand the dog her treat (no later than 1 second or so, the sooner after the mark the better). After you have released her you can touch and praise her, but during the training you should do no more than a soft "Good dog" kind of thing, so you don't excite her into forgetting what she's doing.

Marking a behavior is only used in the beginning stages of learning, to help your dog figure out what you are looking for. Once she has figured it out, you no longer need to mark the behavior. However, if you are working on improving it, you should go back to marking it, since the behavior is now being learned under different circumstances.

For example, once you have taught your dog to sit on command in the kitchen while you are standing in front of her, you don't need to mark the sit anymore. But if you decide to work on getting her to sit on your deck on command, you should go back to marking, since this is a new challenge for her.

Equipment Do's and Don'ts

For this program you will need some basic equipment, nothing fancy or hard to obtain. We do NOT use prong collars or choke collars – the stress of these on a dog's neck can injure her and contribute to aggression when on a walk. We will be teaching your dog to walk nicely on her own rather than using fear of pain to keep her from pulling. And, of course, no shock collars are to be used. This is positive training – we teach our dogs to love working with us.

Here is a list of equipment we will be using in this course:

Collar
You should have a flat buckle or clip collar on your dog at all times, with a tag with the dog's name and your phone number (you may also want your address on the tag) in case your dog bolts out the door and is lost. We will be working with this collar on training leash walking as well.

Harness
For small dogs, any harness will do, but for larger breeds or strong pullers you should purchase a FRONT CLIP HARNESS. At pet stores you can find the "Easy Walk Harness" by Premier, which is okay, but I prefer the "SENSE-ation" or "SENSE-ible" harness which can be found at www.softouchconcepts.com. These are wonderful harnesses that greatly reduce pulling while not hurting your dog at all. The harness should be used whenever you are walking your dog without working on her leash walking skills, to help her understand when she is and is not required to pay more attention to you. Collar = working, harness = more casual.

Leash

You should have a 6 foot regular leather or nylon leash for training. Retractable leashes actually make it much harder to train good leash manners, since they keep tension on the leash all of the time, and we want the dog to learn to keep the leash loose. A 30 or 50 ft "long line" is also a great help in training outdoors.

Mat

You should have a flat mat or blanket or bed (nothing puffy or with sides) to teach your dog to go to a place. It doesn't need to be fancy – really, it should be cheap, just in case your dog decides to chew on it. It should be a bit bigger than the space your dog takes up when she lies down. I have used carpet squares, mats for in front of the sink, towels and very flat dog beds for this.

Tips For Effective Training

If you follow these tips while training your dog, you both will have fun and see great results!

Keep it simple. When training something new, find a place where there will be no distractions for your dog. Pick up any toys, be sure it's quiet and no one else is around. Later you will work on being able to obey under any circumstances, but first you must help the dog understand what you are after. If you've ever tried to do arithmetic in your head while there's a lot of commotion going on around you or people are talking to you, you know what I'm talking about.

Make it fun. The secret to an obedient dog is getting her to actually enjoy doing what you ask. If you think about it, you don't have to beg your dog to chase squirrels – she does it because it's fun for her. If you make training fun and happy, she will begin to feel the same way about doing things you ask.

Keep it short. This goes hand-in-hand with making it fun. No matter how fun something is, it will become a drag if you go beyond what the dog enjoys. Always leave her wanting more. A training session should run from a few minutes to 15 minutes at most. Pay attention to how interested your dog is. If she is acting bored or stressed (wandering off, sniffing at the ground, scratching, yawning, etc.), stop and try again later. It definitely helps if your dog is hungry, so be sure to use those times before meals to train.

Set your dog up for success – don't expect more than she can do. If your dog is just learning how to sit on command in a quiet kitchen, don't take her to the dog park and expect that she can do it there. There is a huge difference for your dog, and she will most likely fail. I will be covering how to grow a behavior gradually so that your dog will be able to do it anywhere, but you must take baby steps. It would be like saying, "Now that you can count, let's try calculus!" Sure, you will someday be able to do calculus if you learn the steps leading to it, but obviously it's too big a jump to do directly. Look at your dog's learning skills as growing from counting to calculus, and don't skip the steps she needs in between.

Remember she's LEARNING, cut her a break. Picture yourself in school. You get an answer right and your teacher praises you. You feel great! Then later you make a mistake, and your teacher calls you an idiot and smacks you across the face. How awful is that! That is what it's like for your dog if you punish her for mistakes when she's just learning things. She will stop enjoying the process and get nervous about making mistakes. A better teacher will simply point out the error and help you to figure out how to do it right next time. Be a good teacher. A mistake just means your dog hasn't quite gotten it yet. This is true of everything from housetraining to coming when called. If your dog isn't doing what you want, accept that she hasn't thoroughly learned it yet and you just need to continue to help her figure out how to do it right.

Try to see it from her point of view. If your dog decided to go chase a bird in the middle of your training session, pay attention to what she's telling you. She's not "blowing you off" – she's telling you that chasing that bird is more important to her than working with you right now. This is valuable information! You now have to think of ways to change her view of working with you so that coming to you is more rewarding/fun/exciting than chasing a bird. Dogs make choices just like people. You want her to make you her choice more and more often. If you follow this program, you'll see that happen.

Use what she does to see where you are. As mentioned above, pay attention to what your dog is telling you. Don't get angry – make a plan! Your dog may love you totally but still prefer to do something else when you call. It's not personal, it's just information. Each time she "disobeys" you, she is telling you where the weak spots in her training are. Just begin to shore those weak spots up, and you'll have a trained dog!

Don't be in a hurry – build strong foundations. As tempting as it may be to try to rush along in your training, it's not a good idea. If you build a very strong response in the early stages, it will be much, much easier for your dog to behave correctly when the situation becomes harder. Take the time to get great responses to easy levels of the commands you teach. Then moving ahead becomes a snap!

Mix training into real life. Be sure to throw some training into all of your interactions with your dog. If you only have training "sessions", your dog will begin to think that those are the only times she needs to give you attention. Before you give her dinner, ask for a sit or down. Before going outside, do a short stay. Make doing things for you perfectly ordinary, and she will learn that this is what life is now – you ask and she does it.

Remember, training is about getting from where you are to where you want to be. Bob Bailey, one of the greatest animal trainers of all time, said something to that effect. If you know where you are, and you know where you want to be, you just need some knowledge and a plan, and practice, practice, practice, and you'll get there. This book will give you the knowledge and the plan. The practice is up to you.

Part III - The Things Your Dog Should Know

1 – Sit

Why do this?

"Sit" is one of the first things most people teach their dogs, and although it is a very simple act, it has many uses. A solid sit on command can help stop a dog jumping up, counter surfing, and being generally obnoxious. You can use it to keep your dog's attention on you when other dogs are walking by. I like to say that when your dog is sitting, she isn't jumping on you, biting your ankles, pulling your clothes, stealing food, chewing your shoes – in short, she simply can't get into trouble while she's in a sit. After you have a strong response to the "Sit" command, you can use it any time you feel the need to get your dog under control, or to remind her to pay attention to you.

Getting the behavior – Hand signal

Begin by getting prepared – be in a quiet room with no distractions, and have tasty treats in your pocket or treat pouch. Put a treat in your hand. Get your dog's attention and start with her standing in front of you. Take the treat and hold it just at her nose, and with her following it, move the treat slightly up and toward her back, easing her into a sit.

Do not say anything as you do this! If you say "Sit", or worse, "Sit, sit, sit", you will just teach her to ignore that sound. Since at this stage, she doesn't even know what you want her to do, keep quiet and simply lure her into a sit. At the instant her bottom hits the floor, say "YES!" and give her the treat. Then say "Okay" and move a bit to show her she can get up.

"Sit" should mean "Sit there until I tell you to do something different", so remember to give it a beginning and an end. Do this a few times until she shows she is starting to understand by easily sitting as you move the treat. Now you must stop using a treat to lure her. Hide a treat in your other hand, and pretend to lure her as you have been doing. Since your hand will still smell like treats and she is expecting to sit down, she will most likely sit the same way she has been while being lured. Say "YES!" and quickly give her the treat from the other hand, then release her with "Okay". Repeat this several times until she shows that she is "getting it" by sitting when you move your hand as if luring (no food in it, remember) 8 times out of 10.

If she stops sitting with your hand signal, use the food lure again once or twice, then go back to using your hand without food. Always have a treat in your other hand so you can quickly reward the correct behavior with an M/T (mark/treat, "YES!" followed by the treat from your other hand).

As she begins to get better at this, begin to wait a bit longer before marking and treating, first one second, then two, etc. If she gets up before you mark or release her, you are extending the time too fast, so shorten the time for a while and then try again.

Getting the behavior – Verbal signal

After your dog is showing that she understands what you mean when you use the hand signal for "Sit" – moving your hand up from her nose – it is time to teach her to respond when you say the word.

KEY POINT: If you say the word at the same time as you give her the signal, she will pay attention to what is easiest for her to figure out (hand signals) and ignore the word.

Dogs are not verbal creatures; rather, they study body language for clues as to what you mean. We must teach them to understand what our sounds mean. So to do this, with a treat hidden in your hand, say the word "Sit" once, wait one second, then give the hand signal. When she sits, M/T and release. Repeat this 10 times, then say "Sit" and wait. Don't give the hand signal this time, just wait and see if she will assume that since every time she heard that sound before you would follow it with the signal for sitting, she might as well just sit.

Give her time to think if she needs it, but don't repeat the command. If she sits, reward her with a jackpot, 3 or 4 treats one right after the other, then release! This is a big step, so celebrate! When she can sit when asked in a quiet room with no distractions 8 times out of 10, then it's time to make things a bit more challenging.

Practicing the behavior

Once she has begun to show that she understands, you will begin to treat her less frequently. Always treat each success at first so that she can figure out that she did the behavior correctly, but once she is showing that she's "getting" it, if you continue to reward every single time she sits when you ask, she will begin to expect a treat and be unhappy if you don't give her one. I liken it to a vending machine versus a slot machine. If you put money into a vending machine and you don't get your candy bar, the very first time it happens, you are angry. Vending machines are predictable and boring, and you only put money in to get something back right now. Slot machines, on the other hand, are unpredictable and exciting. When you put money into one, you don't necessarily expect something back, but you do hope for it. When eventually you hit a jackpot, it's a thrill, even if you've spent more than you won! When your dog looks at working with you as a slot machine, you'll find that she begins to try harder to get you to give that treat rather than being annoyed that she got nothing that time.

You do this by starting to require 2 or 3 good responses before giving a treat. Say "Sit", after she sits, release her, move and ask again, release her, move and ask again, then M/T and release. Vary how many times you want her to sit without a treat – being unpredictable makes you more interesting. Also, notice if she sits unusually quickly – M/T for that every time, maybe even a jackpot! Eventually you won't be treating for sits at all, since she will be excellent at this, and you can save your treats for more challenging successes. Remember the sequence: "Sit", Mark, Treat, "Okay" and move.

Improving the behavior

When you are getting consistently correct responses in a quiet place, it's time to make it a bit harder. This process is called proofing, during which you systematically raise the bar on a behavior with the goal that your dog will be able to perform it correctly in any circumstance. Begin slowly, by simply moving to different rooms in your house and practice the "Sit" sequence. Then find a quiet place outside, preferably a deck or driveway, and try there. Then move to the grass.

Try asking her while you are seated, and again while you are not facing her. Have someone walk past you at a distance as you ask your dog to sit. Ask for a sit when there are several people nearby. On walks, stop and ask for sits periodically. Be sure to reward well whenever you have added a new challenge.

You may have to back up a bit and re-teach things that look different to your dog, but that's part of the process. The more circumstances you practice in, the more likely you are to have a dog who will be able to sit for you no matter when you ask.

Troubleshooting

If you are unable to lure your dog into a sitting position, you may want to try capturing. When you see your dog begin to sit down, say "Sit" and then mark the instant her bottom hits the floor and treat and release as above. Soon she will begin to sit more often in front of you, and then you can try asking for a sit before she begins to do it herself. If she doesn't respond imme-diately, WAIT. Give her time to think – **DO NOT REPEAT THE COMMAND**. If she gets distracted and walks away, go back to capturing for a while. If she thinks for a moment or two and then guesses that you want her to sit down, give her a jack-pot (3-5 little treats in a row) to celebrate her figuring it out.

As you make it a bit harder for her in the "improving the be-havior" stage, be sure to take tiny steps. You want each one to be "Oh, it's just like the one we did before, just a little bit dif-ferent". If she can't respond correctly two times in a row, back up and make it easier for her for a little while, then try again. You may be making too big of a jump between steps, or she may not fully understand what you want yet.

Take it on the road

Once your dog can easily sit on command in different places and under different conditions, remember to practice this everywhere you take her. This is how you will get reliable behavior anywhere – practice, practice, practice.

2 – Down

Why do this?

"Down" is a wonderful help in teaching your dog to be calm. It's harder to jump back up from a down than from a sit, and by working long down-stays, your dog can learn to relax no matter what is going on. You can put your dog in a down while waiting at the vet's office, while you are chatting with someone you ran into on a walk, while you answer the door for a delivery, while you open the oven door – there is no end to the uses for a good solid down.

Getting the behavior – Hand signal

Begin by getting prepared – be in a quiet room with no distractions, and have tasty treats in your pocket or treat pouch. Put a treat in your hand. Get your dog's attention and start with her sitting in front of you. Take the treat and hold it just at her nose, and with her following it, move the treat down and in slightly toward her chest, easing her into a down, which means both ends of the dog are on the ground, butt and elbows. Do not say anything as you do this! If you say "Down", or worse, "Down, down, down", you will just teach her to ignore that sound. Since at this stage, she doesn't even know what you want her to do, keep quiet and simply lure her into a down. At the instant her elbows hit the floor while her butt is still down, say "YES!" and give her the treat. Then say "Okay" and move a bit to show her she can get up.

"Down" should mean "Lie there until I tell you to do something different", so remember to give it a beginning and an end.

Do this a few times until she shows she is starting to understand by easily lying down as you move the treat. Now you must stop using a treat to lure her. Hide a treat in your other hand, and pretend to lure her as you have been doing. Since your hand will still smell like treats and she is expecting to lie down, she will most likely do a down the same way she has been while being lured. Say "YES!" and quickly give her the treat from the other hand, then release her with "Okay". Repeat this several times until she shows that she is "getting it" by lying down when you move your hand as if luring (no food in it, remember) 8 times out of 10.

If she stops lying down with your hand signal, use the food lure again once or twice, then go back to using your hand without food. Always have a treat in your other hand so you can quickly reward the correct behavior with an M/T (mark/treat, "YES!" followed by the treat from your other hand).

As she begins to get better at this, begin to wait a bit longer before marking and treating, first one second, then two, etc. If she gets up before you mark or release her, you are extending the time too fast, so shorten the time for a while and then try again.

Getting the behavior – Verbal signal

After your dog is showing that she understands what you mean when you use the hand signal for "Down" – moving your hand down from her nose – it is time to teach her to respond when you say the word. KEY POINT: If you say the word at the same time as you give her the signal, she will pay attention to what is easiest for her to figure out (hand signals) and ignore the word. Dogs are not verbal creatures; rather, they study body language for clues as to what you mean. We must teach them to understand what our sounds mean.

So to do this, with a treat hidden in your hand, say the word "Down" once, wait one second, then give the hand signal. When she lies down, M/T and release. Repeat this 10 times, then say "Down" and wait. Don't give the hand signal this time, just wait and see if she will assume that since every time she heard that sound before you would follow it with the signal for lying down, she might as well just lie down.

Give her time to think if she needs it, but don't repeat the command. If she lies down, reward her with a jackpot, 3 or 4 treats one right after the other, then release! This is a big step, so celebrate!

When she can lie down when asked in a quiet room with no distractions 8 times out of 10, then it's time to make things a bit more challenging.

Practicing the behavior

Once she has begun to show that she understands, you will begin to treat her less frequently. Always treat each success at first so that she can figure out that she did the behavior correctly, but once she is showing that she's "getting" it, if you continue to reward every single time she lies down, she will begin to expect a treat and be unhappy if you don't give her one. Refer to the "vending machine versus slot machine" discussion in the section on "Sit". You do this by starting to require 2 or 3 good responses before giving a treat. Say "Down", after she lies down, release her, move and ask again, release her, move and ask again, then M/T and release.

Vary how many times you want her to lie down without a treat – being unpredictable makes you more interesting. Also, notice if she responds unusually quickly – M/T for that every time, maybe even a jackpot!

Eventually you won't be treating for lying down at all, since she will be excellent at this, and you can save your treats for more challenging successes. Remember the sequence: "Down", Mark, Treat, "Okay" and move.

Improving the behavior

When you are getting consistently correct responses in a quiet place, it's time to make it a bit harder. This process is called "proofing", during which you systematically raise the bar on a behavior with the goal that your dog will be able to perform it correctly in any circumstance. Begin slowly, by simply moving to different rooms in your house and practice the "Down" sequence. Then find a quiet place outside, preferably a deck or driveway, and try there. Then move to the grass. Try asking her while you are seated, and again while you are not facing her. Have someone walk past you at a distance as you ask your dog to lie down.

Ask for a down when there are several people nearby. On walks, stop and ask for downs periodically. Be sure to reward well whenever you have added a new challenge. You may have to back up a bit and re-teach things that look different to your dog, but that's part of the process. The more circumstances you practice in, the more likely you are to have a dog who will be able to lie down no matter when you ask.

Now that you have two commands that your dog can respond to, begin to mix them up. You may find that she is confused – after all, she's still guessing a lot of the time. She may start to lie down when you ask for a sit, and vice versa. Be patient and work on each command some more, then try mixing them up again. Be sure you don't reward for a mistake – it may seem cute when she sits when asked for a down, but if you reward it, she won't ever be able to figure out the difference. Just move her out of the incorrect position and quietly ask again.

Troubleshooting

Luring a puppy or dog into a down is often a frustrating experience. The front goes down and the back pops up! Keep trying, though, since often you can catch one correct movement, and if you reward that with a jackpot, she will often remember what she did and be able to do it again. If either you or your dog is getting frustrated, you should probably capture the down. When you see your dog begin to lie down, say "Down" and then mark the instant she is lying down, and treat and release as above. Soon she will begin to lie down more often in front of you, and then you can try asking for a down before she begins to do it herself. If she doesn't respond immediately, WAIT.

Give her time to think – **DO NOT REPEAT THE COMMAND**. If she gets distracted and walks away, go back to capturing for a while. If she thinks for a moment or two and then guesses that you want her to lie down, give her a jackpot (3-5 little treats in a row) to celebrate her figuring it out.

As you make it a bit harder for her in the "improving the behavior" stage, be sure to take tiny steps. You want each one to be "Oh, it's just like the one we did before, just a little bit different". If she can't respond correctly two times in a row, back up and make it easier for her for a little while, then try again. You may be making too big of a jump between steps, or she may not fully understand what you want yet.

Take it on the road

Once your dog can easily lie down on command in different places and under different conditions, remember to practice this everywhere you take her. This is how you will get reliable behavior anywhere – practice, practice, practice.

3 – Stay

Why do this?

As mentioned in both "Sit" and "Down", having a dog who will stay in position on command is a critical skill. You can use it to help prevent jumping on guests, to answer the door without your dog trying to get out, to keep your dog away from something dangerous, and to build calm behavior during exciting situations. But to my mind, "Stay" is one of the best ways to build calmness in your dog in any situation.

Frankly, the "Stay" command is redundant – "Sit" means "sit until I tell you to do something else", and "Down" means "lie there until I tell you to do something else", so you don't really need to teach a separate "Stay" command. But most people seem to like to add the extra feeling of control that saying "Stay" gives them, so I will use it here. But feel free to follow these instructions using just "Sit" and "Down" without saying "Stay" if you prefer.

Also, since I am not teaching my pet dog to do competition obedience, I am fine if my dog slides into a down during a stay when I asked for a sit. He isn't that comfortable in a sitting position, and I'm happy that he's settling to stay quietly in either position. If you don't want to do that, then you should require that the dog remain in the position asked.

Getting the behavior

Find a quiet spot for training with no distractions. Hide several treats in your hand. With your dog in either a sit or down position right in front of you, as soon as she looks at you, briefly

39

hold out your empty hand like a traffic cop and quietly say "Stay" once to your dog. Wait one second, then say quietly mark and treat, wait for your dog to look at you again, and repeat the "Stay" process. Do a sequence of three or four stays in a row and then release your dog with "Okay!" and movement.

It's important to speak quietly and not to touch her when rewarding her, or else she may get excited and jump up. After you release her, you can praise and pet her to show her this was really fun. Always sound quiet and calm when asking for "control" behaviors like "Sit", "Down" and "Stay", and be happy and excited for movement behaviors like "Come". By repeating the sequence several times in a row, you are beginning to teach your dog to stay in place longer and wait for you to come back and deliver her reward.

If she gets up, just quietly move her back to the same spot and try again. Shorten the time between saying "Stay" and the mark/treat. After a few tries, wait one second again and see if she can do it. **DO NOT MOVE AWAY FROM YOUR DOG YET!** You are building the foundation for a great stay, so take it slowly and be sure your dog is solid at every step. Initially you are only asking for her to stay put for several one second intervals in a row.

After she is paying good attention to you during this exercise, begin waiting for two seconds sometimes. Then three, but mix it up. When your dog can easily stay for five seconds with you standing in front of her, it's time to move on.

Practicing the behavior

There are three parts to the stay – the three D's of duration (time), distance and distractions. You have begun to build some duration in the beginning stages of this work, and now it's time to add some distance. We will save working around distractions for last, since that is the hardest for any dog to learn.

In a quiet room, have several treats hidden in one hand. Put your dog in a sit or down, and when she looks at you, ask her to "Stay", and take one step back and then right back to the dog.

DO NOT STAY AWAY, JUST BOUNCE RIGHT BACK. Your step back and forth should happen so quickly that you are back before your dog decides to get up and follow you. Some dogs can't help but follow movement, so if she gets up, you just make the exercise easier. You may have to just sway a bit backward and M/T a couple of times, then move your foot a little and M/T, and work up to a full step.

Always make each progression seem very similar to the last one, so your dog can guess easily to just stay put. Once you can reliably move back one step and right back to your dog, work on two steps and right back, then three steps. Mix up how many steps you take during the single stay series.

Remember to do three or four consecutive stays before releasing your dog. At this point, do not turn your back on the dog, just back away from her. Once your dog reliably stays put for you to back up six steps and then go right back to her, it's time to mix time and distance. You've probably noticed that you are asking for longer stays when you step farther back, but now you can begin to move one step back and wait one second before returning.

NOTE: It is very important to return to your dog rather than call her to you at this point. If you call her, you are rewarding her for coming to you rather than for the stay, but more important is that you are teaching her to look forward to being released, when what we really want is for her to relax and enjoy the stay. So be sure to return to her while you build up her ability to stay well. Continue to work with time and distance

41

combinations to improve your dog's stay foundation before beginning the next section - distractions.

Improving the behavior

If you have done your job correctly, you should have a solid foundation of stays from your dog with you backing up for up to six steps while staying away for up to five seconds. It's time to ask for more. Here are the steps for some common distractions for your dog:

Stay while you turn your back – Ask for a "Stay", and while right in front of your dog, quickly turn one quarter way around and then back to your dog to M/T. This is the first time you should be breaking eye contact with her, and you don't want to give her time to think that maybe you don't want her to stay anymore since you aren't looking at her.

Do this several times, then move half way around and right back. After you have practiced this a bit, try turning around and taking one step, then quickly returning to your dog. Build this up until you can walk away from your dog for up to six steps and then return.

Stay while you move in other directions – Follow the same process, only begin to move to the side, starting with only one step and working up to several steps and back. Then begin to walk around the area in front of your dog, starting slowly and working up to more time wandering around in front of her.

Stay while you walk around your dog – First, take a small step to the side of your dog, return and M/T. Then move a bit farther around her, maybe one quarter of the way. Return and M/T. Repeat this a couple of times, then try to go halfway around her and back. If she starts to get up, return and try again going less of the way around a few times. Continue like this until you can go all the way around her. Then begin to work on running around her, starting with a slow jog and working up to running around her for 15 seconds.

Stay while you run away from your dog – Once she is reliably staying while you walk away, begin to slowly jog, and work up to running away for 10 feet or so and then past her 10 feet the other way before returning to M/T.

Stay while you leave the room – Start your stay near a doorway inside your house. First ask for a stay and move near the doorway, return to her and M/T, repeat this, and then go through the doorway part of the way (the dog should still be able to see part of you), and quickly return, M/T and release. Do this sequence a couple of times, then instead of going partway through the door, go all the way and pop right back out. You don't want the dog to have time to wonder if she should follow you. After you've done this a few times, try staying a second or so, and work up to longer. Be sure to move in small increments of difficulty. If she gets up, make it easier a few times and work back to where you had the problems.

Stay while you sit down on a chair – This will almost always cause a dog to break her stay, so you must (as always) break it down into steps. First work on stay while you move toward the chair, then stay while you touch the chair. Next, do a stay while you go over to the chair and make a slight movement toward sitting but you get right back up and go M/T your dog. Then make a bigger movement like starting to sit, and keep doing this until you actually sit and get right up to M/T. Soon you will be able to go and sit down, wait a bit, and return to your dog still in her stay.

Stay while another person walks by – Put your dog in a stay in front of you and have someone the dog knows well walk by well behind you. If this is too hard for your dog, don't wait until they walk all the way past, but M/T several times quickly as they go by to keep your dog's attention on you. Then begin to space out the M/T longer as your dog learns to handle what's happening. When she can stay with you in front of her, have your helper go past progressively closer to your dog, with you maintaining her attention on you. When she can have someone walk right by, begin working on this while you are a step or two away from her.

Stay while you open the door – This is very difficult for most dogs, so don't start working on it until you have excellent stays with easier distractions. Put your dog in a stay, then go to the door and return without touching it to M/T. Do this a few times. If your dog is solid with this, then go and touch the handle and return to M/T. Now turn the handle without opening the door. Turn the handle, open the door a tiny bit and quickly close it and return. Continue making small changes until you can open the door all the way, wait for a few seconds, close it and then return to M/T.

Stay during noises – Put your dog in a stay and clap your hands lightly, M/T. Then clap several times, M/T. Move away from the dog and knock on the wall, return and M/T. Leave the room, clap lightly, return and M/T. Continue working with various noises such as bells, clangs, talking, singing, being sure that your dog can succeed before moving on to harder distractions. Have a helper ring the doorbell while she is in a stay right in front of you, then work on being farther away from her. Doorbells are extremely hard, as your dog has no doubt learned that it always brings excitement. Don't open the door at first, just M/T if your dog can stay while hearing the doorbell ring. This would be a good place to use your very best treats.

Stay during other distractions – Hopefully you are getting the pattern here: start with the easiest version of what you want and slowly work up harder and harder versions of it. It really doesn't take long to do this if you have built a proper foundation during your early work. You dog will be able to easily understand that each step is like the prior one, and you can move through the process very quickly. Just pick the situation you want to have your dog stay during, break it down and practice each step until she can do it before moving on to the next one.

Troubleshooting

If your dog gets up, make it easier. In the beginning, you may just have to spend some time practicing stays with your dog right in front of you. Once she "gets" it, you can move along pretty quickly. If you still have too much trouble, you may not be in a quiet enough location. Go somewhere where there is nothing at all interesting to the dog. Also, if your dog is in a very excited state, wait until she is calmer to work on this. She may not be able to focus if she is all worked up.

Whenever you reach a point where she can't hold her stay, back up to an easier version of the same stay, practice that for a few tries, and then try again to get the harder stay. If things are going badly, don't keep trying – ask for something she can definitely do right, reward her cheerfully, and go back to this exercise later. Don't make it a grind for either of you.

Take it on the road

The more scenarios you work on systematically with your dog, the more reliable her stay will become. You will also find that she can handle situations you didn't work on after a while, since she has really figured out that "Stay" means "stay put no matter what's going on".

Work on short easy stays wherever you take your dog. This is one of the best things you can teach her. As she gets better at this, you can reward her more with praise and petting than treats, but for really hard things, use treats sometimes – it's a great bonus to keep up your dog's enthusiasm for working with you.

4 – Come

Why do this?

I'm sure it's pretty obvious that this is one of the most important things you can teach your dog, but it may not be as obvious why it is one of the hardest things to teach well. If you think about it, you are asking your dog to leave anything at all, no matter how interesting or exciting, just because you called her.

In order to get this kind of response, you will have to work on making coming to you just about the best experience your dog can have. Some people are lucky, and their dog feels that way almost without trying, but for most of us, a lot of time and practice is necessary to get a reliable recall (dogtrainer-speak for the "Come" command). Since having a reliable recall can save your dog's life, it is time well invested.

A couple of things to remember when working on recalls: 1) never call your dog if you are sure she won't come; 2) never let your dog off-leash in an unenclosed area until you have proven without a doubt that your dog will come under ANY conditions, or you are risking her life; 3) after you praise and treat her for coming, send her off to play most of the time, so she doesn't think that you are ending her play when you call; and 4) as always, start easy and work up to harder situations as your dog is able to handle them.

Getting the behavior

The best way to work on getting your dog to love coming to

47

you is to play recall games. By having your dog come to you for fun and treats, she will begin to love running to you, and you will be most of the way there.

Chase Me Game – This is a game one person can play with a dog anytime they are in a safe, enclosed area such as in the house or in a fenced yard. Have some tasty treats in one hand. Get your dog's attention and toss a treat behind you (to give you a head start), saying "Get It!", and as she eats the treat, run quickly in the opposite direction, calling her in a fun, happy voice. Be silly, slap your legs, make funny noises – anything that your dog thinks is fun and will help her run after you.

When she reaches you, stop and praise and give her a treat. Always be sure to give her the treat very close to you, and grab her collar at the same time to get her used to the fact that you might grab her after calling. It does no good to teach your dog to come and stay just out of reach, so insist that she comes all the way so that you can grab her, and then let go, toss another treat behind you and play again. Play this a few times in a row, but don't play so much that your dog gets bored. Always leave her wanting to play more.

Back and Forth Game – This is the two or more person version of the Chase Me Game. Start with two people around 6 feet apart in a quiet enclosed area. Each person should have some tasty treats hidden in their hand. The first person should call the dog in a happy, fun voice, and run away a little to encourage the dog to chase him. When she arrives, treat her close in with a grab of her collar, and while she's eating, the next person should call her the same way.

Soon your dog will be happily running back and forth for fun and treats. You can add other people to this game now, calling the dog to each of you in random order. Be sure this is fun and happy and you stop before your dog gets bored.

48

Go and Come Game – toss a treat as you point away from yourself, saying "Go!". As soon as your dog arrives and is eating the treat, call her back to you. When she arrives, give her a collar grab and another treat, and repeat. After you've done this a number of times, try just making the motion while saying "Go!", and if she moves away from you, throw the treat out ahead of her. This will give you a new command to move her in the direction you point.

Practicing the behavior

The more you play these games, the easier it will be to get your dog to love being called. But keep in mind that if you call her for unpleasant things like nail trimming, to come in when playing outside, to scold her for something, or to take something she wants away from her, you will be undermining the work you are doing. It's better to go get her than to call her for these things.

Be sure to vary the location so that she gets used to coming happily in many places. Begin to play hide-and-seek with your dog, and have a big party when she finds you! You want your dog to hear you call and think, "Oh, wow, I LOVE this game!!!"

Improving the behavior

As you see your dog responding well in more places, take the 1000 Recall Challenge, which is to call your dog 1000 times in one month. This comes out to just over 30 a day, which when you think about how long it takes to play the Back and Forth Game, you can see it doesn't have to be a big production. But you need to call and reward your dog in many different ways to have this be effective.

If your dog is in another room, call her, have a party. Play the Chase Me Game a few times. Hide from your dog and call her. Call her from different rooms, and from different parts of the yard, if it's fenced. Occasionally play tug when she arrives instead of giving her treats all the time. The more variety the better.

Be sure to have a party and/or treats EVERY SINGLE TIME. You are building an automatic response in your dog that you will need if she is ever to come back when she sees something like a squirrel.

Troubleshooting

If your dog is ignoring you, move to a more boring location and use better treats. Sometimes when playing the Back and Forth Game, a dog will decide to just stay with one person and hope they give her another treat. First, be sure that both people have the same treats. The person where the dog is stuck should totally ignore her, just look at the ceiling, while the other person can move a bit closer, slap his leg, make kissy noises and run from her going "Woo hoo" or some other silly sound.

Don't keep calling her, and especially don't wave treats in front of you to get her to come – then she will learn to look for the treats and if she doesn't see them, may decide to ignore you. Treats are a reward AFTER she arrives. If she consistently ignores one person, they should spend some time playing the Chase Me Game and Come and Go Game with no one else around, and also work on leash attention (see Behavior 10). If you are totally being ignored, take your treats and go away. Try again when your dog is hungry.

Take it on the road

Now it's time to put your dog on a "long line", which is a light leash that's anywhere from 15 to 50 feet long. You can buy them in the training section of most pet stores. For small dogs you might need to use a very light clothesline tied to a leash clip (you can get both at most hardware stores). Let your dog drag it around a fenced yard for a while so that she doesn't really notice it anymore.

Later when you are in an unfenced area, if your dog is slow moving, you can just let the line drag, but if you have a fast dog that is likely to chase a squirrel or another dog, you can tie the line to your waist. Just be very careful – it's easy to trip or catch your fingers in a line.

With a long line on your dog, you can practice anywhere – outside your front door is a great place to work, since if your dog gets out the door, you want her to know that she comes back when you call. Take her to fields, friends' yards, parks – anywhere you can. If she ignores you in favor of something else, such as a squirrel or other person or dog, gently stop her, walk over to her (please don't reel her in) and take the line near her and lead her back somewhere farther away from the distraction to make it easier for her to obey.

Keep increasing distance until she can ignore the distraction and come to you. Don't make a big deal out of this – it's not a failure, it's information about what she can and can't handle, so that you know what you need to work on still. If this sounds like a lot of work, it is. But if you keep it fun for both of you, you'll see your dog get better and better at coming under all conditions. When working outside in areas with squirrels, dogs and people, be sure to use super great treats.

Getting a fantastic recall is one of dog training's biggest challenges. If you want to do more intensive work on this command, I recommend you read my book "COME HERE! Teach Your Dog to Come When You Call", available at Amazon.com.

5 – Walking Nicely on Leash

Why do this?

If you have a small dog, you may not feel the need to work on this, but if you have a large or strong dog, this is a must. Personally, I think it's a good idea to teach all dogs to walk politely on the leash. A walk shouldn't be about how many trees to sniff or how much is going on around you – it should be about being together. Once on the leash, most dogs treat their owners as a dead weight to be pulled around as fast as possible. And while we understand that we walk so much slower than our dogs (for the most part), we need to teach them to respect that this is how we walk, and to learn to enjoy walking with us.

In conjunction with "Let's Go" for leash walking, we should also teach "Go Sniff" to allow our dog to be free to sniff around for a minute or two before resuming our walk. Note: if you truly wish to teach your dog to walk nicely, you need to commit to yourself that you will never let her pull you anywhere again. If she pulls in one direction, you will reverse and gently bring her with you (no yanks or jerks, please).

As mentioned in the equipment section, I recognize that there are times when you simply have to walk the dog and don't have time to do it right. If you use a harness (front-clip for strong pullers) when you aren't working, and the collar for when you are, it will help your dog understand when she can and can't pull, although the less pulling you allow the faster you will see results.

Getting the behavior

The first step in leash walking is to teach your dog to acknowledge you while on the leash. In a quiet spot (indoors is best at first), attach your dog's leash to her collar, have some treats hidden in your hand, and stand still. Wait for your dog to look at you, and when she does, say "Yes!" and give her a treat. For some dogs, you may have to wait a while, but eventually almost every dog will get bored and look at you like "What the heck is this about?" Say "Yes!" and give her a treat.

If your dog is refusing to look at you, either you are not in a boring enough spot, or she doesn't care about your treats. Fix whichever it is, and try again. If she pulls, just hold firm – don't pull her back or jerk her. Now that she is looking at you (some dogs just start to stare), instead of handing her the treat, drop it on the floor next to you and take a step away, facing her. Now she will have to look down to get her treat and then look to see where you went. When she looks at you, say "Yes!" and drop another treat next to you and move away again. Practice this until your dog is easily following you even if you move several steps.

Be sure you are still facing her when you move away, and keep the leash short enough that your dog won't get her feet tangled in it. You have now taught her that you matter to her even though she is on the leash, a good beginning.

Practicing the behavior

Now that you are walking backwards with your dog following you, begin to pivot around so that you are still walking in the same direction but now the dog is beside you instead of in front of you. Give her a treat while you are walking forward together. Take only a step or two like this and pivot back to the original position. Continue walking, switching back and forth between backwards and forwards (the dog is always facing forward, either in front of you or beside you).

As you practice this, spend longer stretches with the dog by your side, treating every couple of steps. If she begins to pull, immediately say her name and then gently draw her back to you (you should be walking backward again), and then try again. Keep saying her name and moving away until she finally turns toward you, then say "Good girl!" and reward her.

You want saying her name to warn her that you are about to pull her away. Eventually she will figure you're going to pull her away anyway, so she might as well not bother to pull. If your dog can't walk past something without pulling, move farther away from it.

Improving the behavior

Start to say "Let's Go" when you begin walking now. Begin to work on this in a slightly more interesting area, like a driveway or patio (not on the grass at this point, too much to sniff). If she can follow/walk with you here, good. If not, find a slightly easier place or work when she is hungrier. Continue to lead her around like this for longer stretches, still alternating following and walking by your side.

When you want her to be able to take a break, she must not be pulling before you release her. When she is not pulling you, say "Go Sniff" and move with her to an interesting place. Give her a moment or two to check it out, and then say "Let's Go!" and begin your walk again. If she doesn't want to go, say her name and then gently draw her with you (no yanks or jerks).

If you see she wants to go sniff somewhere, you can let her (tell her to go sniff first – this should be a gift from you) provided she doesn't pull you. If she does, you can back away from the distraction and try again (a lot like the greeting exercises below), and only let her go if she isn't pulling you.

You can choose to use treats to help keep your dog's attention on walks for a while, or you can just use forward movement as the reward. See which works best for you. As she gets better and better, spend less time walking backward, using this only if she gets ahead of you and begins to pull (remember, say her name and then draw her gently back toward you).

Troubleshooting

If your dog isn't paying any attention to you while on the leash, you must move to a more boring spot to start working, and increase the value of the treats you are using. If you have to, don't feed your dog breakfast and work on this later in the day so she is really hungry. Be sure to spend a good bit of time with your dog following you while you walk backward before expecting her to stay with you. Always say her name and then back slowly away from anything she pulls toward. When she finally turns toward you, say "Good girl" and reward her, then go a different direction if there is something too hard for her ahead of you.

Take it on the road

Practice walking for longer periods of time, in as many places as you can. Be sure you are "with" your dog – that is, paying attention to her, so that when she pays attention to you, you notice it and reward her with a "Good girl" and/or a treat. If she pulls, always say her name and move gently away from the distraction until she can focus on you again, then praise her and try again. If you are fully committed to not allowing pulling, she will get the message much more quickly than if you let her pull sometimes. Consistency is key, or she will just check to see if it's okay this time rather than just figure there's no point in even trying, since it never gets her to anything. Be sure to give frequent "Go sniff" breaks to keep her from being frustrated by never getting to check anything out.

6 – Leave It

Why do this?

When you are walking down the street with your dog and she sees a dead mouse, "Leave It" is a most handy command. If she has that look in her eye when she sees a shoe on the floor, a good "Leave It" will save everyone grief. You can use "Leave It" for pulling towards other dogs while on a walk, for counter-surfing, to keep her from eating something you dropped on the floor such as medication, and to generally let her know something is off-limits.

Getting the behavior

The key to teaching "Leave It" is to have control over what happens. If you can't stop your dog from getting the object you are asking her to leave, you won't be able to explain what you want, and she may learn the wrong lesson – like, "If I'm faster and sneakier, I can have that thing anyway!" Not what you want to teach.

Stage One: Start with some treats hidden in your hand and your dog on the leash. Toss a treat a couple of feet in front of the dog (where she cannot reach it), say "Leave It" one time only, and hold onto her. **DO NOT LET HER GET THE TREAT!** She will pull for a while, some dogs a long while and others not so long, but will eventually get frustrated and look away from the treat. At that **INSTANT OF DECISION**, say "YES!" and back away from the dog, encouraging her to come with you and give her a treat, preferably a better one than the one you tossed. You must capture that decision point and move the dog away from the "Leave It" object to treat her – this ex-

59

ercise is not about dragging your dog away from something, but rather having her learn to leave it alone when you tell her to. Practice this until she no longer tries to get the treat you tossed. At this point, switch to tossing an object instead of a treat, using the same procedure.

Stage Two: Without your dog around (or have a helper), place an interesting object on the grass a few feet from the sidewalk where you will walk your dog. With your dog on the leash, begin to walk down the sidewalk toward where the object is, and as your dog notices it, say "Leave It" and hold her still until she looks away from it. IMMEDIATELY say "YES!" and hustle down the sidewalk past the object and give her a treat. Don't leave her near the object or she will just try to get it again. As she looks away, you want to get her attention on you. If this is horribly difficult for your dog, either switch to a less interesting object or move it farther away from the sidewalk. As she improves, gradually move it closer and/or use more compelling objects for this.

Practicing the behavior

After she has gotten an understanding of what you mean by "Leave It", you should start using it whenever you are out for a walk. Some of the times you see something of interest to your dog, do a "Leave It" exercise. If your dog is counter-surfing, set up tempting traps on tables and counters and walk past with her on leash. In this case I would have "Leave It" be a default behavior – one that should be automatic and you don't give a command for, i.e. see food on table or counter, don't take it no matter what. Be sure to just hold her still until she makes the decision to stop trying to get the food, then move away quickly and reward her. Be lavish with praise and rewards, and practice every chance you get. To do this without a leash, be sure you or someone else can rescue the food in case she decides to try for it. If she does, move the food farther away and try again, and work towards harder and harder situations.

Improving the behavior

In the house, you can begin to work on food near your dog. When your dog is lying down, place a small treat a little away from her, say "Leave It", and then be prepared to quickly cover the treat if she tries to get it. Some of the time you can give her the treat if she doesn't try for it (especially if she looks at you as if for permission), and other times take it away and give her something else. You can work up to placing the treats very near, or even on, her feet and she won't take them. It's a good party trick to show how you can line treats up your dog's legs and she won't touch them, but more importantly, you are on your way to much better control of what your dog will try to eat. Begin to drop food near her (be ready to step on it if she tries to get it) to teach her that something dropped on the floor isn't automatically hers. As mentioned before, this can save her life if you should accidentally drop a pill on the floor.

Troubleshooting

If your dog is somehow getting to the "Leave It" object, move farther away and keep a tight grip on the leash. If she can't stop staring at it, don't get so close – it's too hard for her. Get to where she can easily give it up to look at you before trying to move close again. You want to set her up for success, so don't make things too hard for her until she's ready. And especially don't let her get the food or object – she will not learn the lesson that you mean to teach.

Take it on the road

Practice "Leave It" when on walks, with all sorts of objects, in all sorts of places. The more you vary the exercise, the easier it is for her to understand that you mean to turn away from the object no matter where or what it is. As she gets better and better at this, you can stop treating her for good choices and reward her with praise and petting.

7 – Take It

Why do this?

When you teach the "Take It" command, you are showing your dog that she is not allowed to grab anything out of your hand – she must have permission first. This cuts down on puppy play-biting, accidental bites during games, and is an important part of playing tug-of-war with any dog. You can use this to give permission for your dog to have something after you have told them to "Leave It" as well.

Getting the behavior

Take a long tug toy or dangly soft toy in both hands. Wave the center at your dog. If she grabs or jumps at it, quickly lift it up out of reach, and when she sits in front of you, wave it again. Don't ask for a sit, just wait until she does it. Continue to wave/remove until she can sit for about one second (less if this is really hard for her), then say "Take It" and let her play tug or chase it with you wiggling it for a minute. If she has it, use the "Drop It" command as described below to get it away from her, and repeat the wave/remove until she sits politely for a second or so, then play again. After a couple of times of play, when you take the toy, give her a treat and put the toy away for next time. Don't leave it with the dog – it's your toy.

Practicing the behavior

Begin to wait for longer self-control from your dog before

playing. Work up slowly to where you can dangle the toy in front of her nose, and even touch her with it and she doesn't grab until told. Use different toys to help her understand that she shouldn't grab anything without permission.

Improving the behavior

Once she solidly understands not to grab toys, start working with other items, like old dish towels (something you don't care about in case she grabs it anyway). You want to teach her that she shouldn't grab anything, not just toys, and so to reward her, give her a treat for not grabbing rather than telling her to take something that's not a toy. This is a good exercise to help with dogs that bite hands and clothing.

Troubleshooting

Some dogs simply won't take something from you. If this is the case with your dog, just try to get her to play with the toy, even if you have to toss it for her. If you have a fast or strong dog, raise the toy high above your head so there is no chance the dog can get it. If your dog is having trouble with this, don't wait long – start giving the "Take It" command after any hesitation at all, and work up to longer waits. Always work where the dog can do what you ask. Use common sense if you feel that your dog could hurt you – don't put yourself at risk.

Take it on the road

Use every opportunity to practice patient waiting for things. Wait for your dog to sit before throwing a ball. Wave the ball in her face to test that she won't try to grab for it. If your dog is ball-crazy, be sure to carefully work up to this, or you may get bitten. By doing this exercise carefully you will prevent bites like that. You want patient control any time your dog wants something.

8 – Drop It

Why do this?

You can use the "Drop It" command anytime you want to get something out of your dog's mouth. Wrestling something from her mouth may cause her to bite, and can also lead to her feeling she needs to guard things from you, which can be dangerous. Teaching the "Drop It" command correctly helps your dog feel that letting go of objects is no problem for her.

Getting the behavior

While playing tug with your dog, stop moving the toy (but still hold onto it), say "Drop It" firmly, and with your other hand, place a yummy treat directly on your dog's nose. As she drops the toy to get the treat, say "Yes!" and give the treat to her. After a few tries, wait a second after saying "Drop It" before putting the treat on her nose to see if she will drop the toy when you ask. If so, wonderful! – have a puppy party with a jackpot of 3 or 4 treats in a row. If not, put a treat on her nose again and keep trying. If she isn't dropping the toy, your treat isn't good enough, so try something better.

Practicing the behavior

Use "Drop It" every time you play tug with your dog, and begin to use it if she has something in her mouth that you don't want her to have. Always be sure to trade a treat for the object until she is excellent at this behavior. You want her to feel good about giving things up.

Improving the behavior

Have play sessions where you quickly do multiple "Take It/Drop It" sequences. Try to make it so that taking and dropping are fun parts of the game.

Troubleshooting

If your dog is refusing to drop things when you put a treat on her nose, switch to a super high value treat, which for most dogs would be meat or cheese. If this doesn't work, only try this when she has something that is not especially valuable to her. Never try to force her to let go unless it is critical to get the object away from her. If she growls at you, stop trying to get her to let go, and use a better reward next time. You must make the reward better than what the dog has in her mouth. For safety, never force a growling dog – she is warning you that she may bite. Back off and work on it another time, making it easier for her.

Take it on the road

Whenever you are out and your dog picks up a stick or other object you don't want her to have, ask her to "Drop It" and reward her for a good choice. You may need extra good treats while outside initially. If you work at this, you soon won't need treats but can praise and pet your dog for doing a good job. When playing tug, switch back and forth between "Take It" and "Drop It" to help build good responses. Tug is good for this, because you can give the item right back to her, helping her to see that there is no real loss here.

9 – Go To Mat

Why do this?

There are many times when you may need your dog to get out of your way and stay there – when someone comes to the door, when you open the oven, while you're eating, or just as a good place to stay and chew on toys while you have visitors. Sometimes people take the mat with them to the vet's office or other potentially scary places as a way for their dog to have a familiar place to wait, which helps calm them. A small flat mat (not a lumpy dog bed) is an easy target for your dog to aim for, much easier than a designated spot on the floor.

Getting the behavior

To teach this, have tasty treats handy. Put the mat on the floor a foot or so away from you, say "Go To Your Mat" (or just "Mat" or whatever you prefer), make a swooping motion toward the mat while letting a treat drop on it from the hand that's swooping. When your dog goes to the mat to get the treat, say "Yes!" and give her another when she's on the mat. To get her off the mat to try again, say "Okay", toss a treat a few feet away and say "Get It". Then say "Go To Your Mat" and swoop another treat onto the mat, treat and get her off again. Repeat this a few times, and then do exactly the same thing only don't toss the treat while swooping your hand toward the mat.

If your dog goes to the mat to look for the treat, then say "Yes!" and give her a jackpot of three or four treats in a row before getting her off to do it again. Get rid of the "lure" treat as soon as possible – you want her to follow your hand, not a treat, except in the beginning to give her the idea of what you want.

Practicing the behavior

Once she is easily going to the mat from a foot or so away, begin to ask from farther away. Be sure to say "Go To Your Mat" before you do the hand motion towards the mat, so that eventually you can just say the command without the hand cue. Be sure to release her to get up – you want to be able to tell her to go there and have it mean "stay there until I tell you otherwise". If she gets confused or doesn't go to her mat, just wait while pointing at it and see if she can figure it out. Don't keep repeating the command. If she loses focus, wait until you have her attention, move a bit closer and try again.

Improving the behavior

First start to wait for her to sit on the mat before rewarding her (don't ask her to sit, just wait, and she will probably sit or lie down, which is also fine). Then move the mat to another location before sending her to it. Sometimes a dog learns to go to the spot rather than the mat, so you may have to re-teach the behavior a few times to help her understand that it's the mat, not the spot, that you want her to go to. Be sure not to reward her simply because she tried or was cute – she won't be able to figure out what you want if you do that. Move the mat around the room and into other rooms. Take the mat outside and teach her to go to it outside as well. Be sure to remember to release her.

Troubleshooting

If your dog isn't following a treat to the mat, stand closer to it. If she just puts one foot on it, give her a jackpot and then start rewarding her for getting closer and closer to what you want, until she is running to the mat. If she seems afraid of the mat, you may need to try a different one – even a small towel will do. Don't use puffy dog beds since they make it more difficult for the dog to just walk onto them. Most dogs pick this one up very quickly, but if not, just take it slow. Don't allow yourself to get frustrated – just take the mat away and try again later.

Take it on the road

Start encouraging your dog to stay on the mat for longer periods of time. Train this like the "Stay" – go over to her and give her a treat every few seconds at first, then take longer. Give her new toys after she goes to her mat. Encourage her to chew on bones on her mat. Eventually work on having her stay on her mat while you eat supper or watch a TV show.

10 – Polite Greetings

Why do this?

Although a tiny puppy jumping on you may seem cute, it isn't cute once she's grown up, and even a small dog can tear up panty hose, so polite greetings are a must. Plus, some people are frightened of dogs, so you don't want them to have to worry about your over-enthusiastic dog leaping on them. This is like most training – you only get out what you put in, so the more people you can practice on, the more likely it is that your dog can learn what to do, and be able to do it.

Getting the behavior

You will need a helper, preferably someone your dog already knows, so it won't be too hard for her. Have treats hidden in your hand and your dog on the leash. Start with your helper about 10 feet away from you and your dog. Put your dog near your side in a sit. Have the helper walk toward your dog, and the instant your dog gets up, the helper should move away again. Do this little dance – helper forward when dog is sitting, backward when dog gets up – until your dog is still able to sit when the helper arrives. The helper can reach to pet your dog at this point, which normally makes her jump up. If that happens, the helper should quickly back away from the dog again, not approaching until she sits again.

You want it to look as if the dog has control over the situation – by sitting she can move the helper closer, by getting up she pushes him away. When the helper finally can pet the dog, he should only stay a second or so, then you treat your dog while he moves away. Repeat this until the helper can walk right up to your dog, pet her, and walk away, and your dog stays sitting the whole time. Your job is to simply hold the dog by your side and treat her as the helper leaves after petting her.

Don't pull her, jerk her or say anything to her, just hold the leash firmly so she can't go anywhere. Let her learn what to do by what happens with the helper. Notice we are not giving a command for this – we want our dog to sit and wait nicely every time someone approaches, without having to tell her. When she gets up, don't reprimand her – let her learn by what happens.

Practicing the behavior

Now that your dog is beginning to understand how to control another person's approach, you need to practice on everyone you can. If you dog goes crazy when your spouse or kids come home, put her on leash and practice with them. From now on, you should never allow your dog to just jump all over people when they come in the door. If you don't have time to work on it, or the person coming in isn't someone who would help with this, put your dog in her crate or another room. Don't let her practice behavior you are trying to get rid of.

Improving the behavior

After you have gotten good results from someone approaching your dog, it's time to turn it around and work on you approaching someone instead. Have your helper (someone the dog knows) stand still 10 feet away, and you take a step towards him. If your dog runs ahead, you simply step back to where you started and gently draw your dog back to you. If 10 feet seems too close, start farther apart. If your dog doesn't pull ahead, continue moving towards the helper. Anytime your dog begins to pull ahead, simply back up and gently tow her back to the starting point. Eventually you will make it all the way to your helper. If your dog doesn't sit, but instead begins to jump, move back away from the helper a few feet and try again. If your dog is too excited at this point, go all the way back to the starting point. With patience, you will be able to walk up to the helper, your dog will sit to get petted and a treat, and you will turn and go. If at any point your dog jumps up, remove her from the helper. Once you can do this with someone familiar, start working with other helpers, and eventually strangers to the dog. Again, we are not giving a command for this – we want our dog to walk nicely and sit every time she approaches someone, without having to tell her. When she starts to pull, don't reprimand her – let her learn by what happens.

Troubleshooting

If your dog gets too excited to be able to greet someone at first, then work on walking past them while you give treats to make it easier. Start at a distance your dog can handle, even if it's 50 feet away, and work closer gradually. Eventually your dog will understand what you want from her and be able to calm down more when people are around. Don't, don't, don't allow her to jump all over anyone from now on. Keep her crated or in another room until things quiet down, then bring her out on leash. Don't let her loose until she calms down.

Take it on the road

Every time you approach someone on a walk or someone comes to your home, you should go through this process until you can see that she has learned to go up and sit whenever she wants to greet someone. The more people you work with, the faster this will happen.

Part IV – Summary

Each of these ten commands serves an important function in a good pet dog. By teaching your dog to listen to you and do what you ask, your dog will learn to settle down faster and be less likely to get into trouble. You will have tools to use when greeting people and other dogs, to stop counter-surfing, shoe-stealing, play biting and jumping on you. Your dog will learn to walk nicely with you on leash, and to lie quietly on her mat while you eat dinner.

Remember I mentioned that dog training is a lot like learning a musical instrument – you get nowhere if you don't practice. If you follow these instructions carefully, moving at a speed that your dog can handle, you will find her ability to listen to you and do what you ask improving weekly. Keep with it, and you will soon have a dog to be proud of!

Appendix A - Benefits of Record Keeping

Keeping track of your training sessions has many benefits: you have a clear record of your progress, so if you are feeling like you're getting nowhere, you can go back and see just how far you have actually come; you can spot specific trouble areas that you may not have noticed before; you can make sure that you work consistently with your dog; and you can easily chart the path from where you are to where you want to be.

Most people don't keep good records, but if you do, you'll find your training efforts will pay off more quickly, since they will help so much with consistency in both what you are doing and how often you are doing it.

I urge you to give it a try – for each session note the date, what you are working on, how many trials you did, what went right, what went wrong, and what is your plan for next time. Then the next time, quickly look over this sheet to see what you wanted to do as your starting point for that session. You'll be amazed at the progress you can make this way.

Appendix B – Glossary

Clicker Training: A method of training new behaviors using a clicker (a small noise maker) to mark the exact behavior that you are rewarding her for. This is used to help a dog understand what you want from her, and is not needed once she is responding well to your request.

Distractions: Things that may make your dog lose focus or decide not to obey you. When first teaching any behavior, you should make sure there are no distractions around. This includes other people, noises, interesting smells, toys nearby, commotion in the vicinity, etc. Once your dog is reliably obeying without distractions, then you begin "proofing", or carefully adding distractions to teach your dog that she can still listen when something else is around.

Jackpot: A special reward of 3 to 4 treats giving quickly one after another, in order to let your dog know that she has done something great! Times to use this would include the first time she does something correctly, when she has ignored a particularly difficult distraction, or just to surprise her and keep it fun.

Marker Training: Same as clicker training, only we use a word, such as "Yes!" to mark the correct behavior. Clicker trainers still use a marker word sometimes, since they may not always have a clicker on them. This is generally not quite as effective as a clicker, since your word can sound different each time, but is usually fine.

M/T: Mark (click or say "Yes!") and give the dog a treat.

Positive Reinforcement Training: Training which uses the scientific laws of learning by focusing on rewarding behaviors that you like and want to see again, and by ignoring or replacing behaviors that you don't like and want to eliminate. By using treats, games, and "real life" rewards we can influence how a dog behaves, and build new habits.

Proofing: The process of systematically working with your dog through more and more difficult distractions in order to be sure she can respond correctly no matter what is going on around her. Proofing should be done by carefully adding one distraction at a time, and working with that until your dog is able to ignore it, then moving on. Eventually you should be training around multiple distractions at the same time, but you must work up to this, or your dog will not be able to succeed.

Reinforcer: Rewards, such as food, games, going outside, getting in a car, taking a walk, belly rubs – anything a dog likes enough to be willing to do things for. Also called a motivator. Be sure the dog likes it – it's not a reinforcer if she doesn't care about it, even if you think it should be.

Reward: Reinforcer.

Setting the dog up for success: When training, be sure that you don't move too fast for your dog, or she won't be able to be correct. When this happens often, she isn't getting enough feedback to know what you actually want from her, since you can't reward her, and you run the risk of getting frustrated. Step back and make it easier until she can reliably be correct, and then make the situation just a bit harder for her. If she can't focus on training, ask for something really easy, reward her, and stop for the time being. If you feel yourself getting frustrated, back up, get a good response to reward, and stop. Training should be fun for both of you – if it's not that day, just stop and try later.

Afterword

FREE BONUS! Be sure to go to

www.ReallySimpleDogTraining.com/DTBonus.html

to get your FREE printable quick reference sheet. This lets you print any or all of the instructions for each command so that you don't have to refer to your book while training.

I wish you the best in your efforts to train your dog. If you diligently follow the steps outlined above, you should see positive results quickly. Just remember that you are teaching your dog a new way to live, and that this takes time. Patience and a sense of humor are your best tools!

If you enjoyed this booklet, I invite you to write a short review on Amazon to help others find success in their training endeavors. Also I recommend checking out my booklet, "Housetraining Success Formula: 6 Simple Steps to Housetraining Your Puppy or Dog" for Amazon Kindle.

If you feel you are ready for more intensive training with your puppy, be sure to take a look at "COME HERE! Teach Your Dog To Come When You Call". This is advanced training in recalling, leash walking, "Leave It" work, and teaches an "Emergency Down". These are skills that can save your dog's life!

Be sure to look for my upcoming booklets in the series "Really Simple Dog Training", coming soon!

Carol Miller, CDT

Claim Your Free Bonus

FREE BONUS! Be sure to go to

http://www.ReallySimpleDogTraining.com/DTBonus.html

to get your FREE printable quick reference guide. This lets you print any or all of the lessons so that you don't have to refer to your book while training. Also be sure to print out your work-sheets from Week One.

About the Author

Carol Miller is a Certified Dog Trainer, and an honors graduate of the Animal Behavior College. In addition to her series of dog training books (Really Simple Dog Training), she has written several children's books about nature and the world we live in.

She lives in New Jersey with her family, which includes two rescued Border Collies and 3 rescued cats.

Learn more about "Really Simple Dog Training" at

www.ReallySimpleDogTraining.com

CPSIA information can be obtained at www.ICGtesting.com
Printed in the USA
LVOW10s0352290414

383646LV00010B/333/P

9 781494 403492